WHITE FANG

RETOLD BY PAULINE FRANCIS

Evans

EVANS BROTHERS LIMITED

Published by Evans Brothers Limited
2A Portman Mansions
Chiltern Street
London W1U 6NR

© Evans Brothers Limited 2003
First published 2003

Printed in Hong Kong

British Library Cataloguing in Publication data
Francis, Pauline
          White fang
          1. Wolfdogs – Canada – Juvenile fiction 2. Children's stories
          I. Title II. London, Jack, 1876 – 1916
          823.9'14 [J]

ISBN 0237525321

WHITE FANG

Introduction

Jack London was born in 1876, in the American State of Pennsylvania. At the age of fifteen, he left home to travel around North America, living the life of a tramp. Then he decided to study at the University of California.

Jack left university because he was caught up in the excitement of the gold rush in the 1890s. Gold had been discovered in the River Klondike, in the Yukon Territory of Northwest Canada. Thirty thousand people travelled to this area (London called it the 'Northland'), hoping to make their fortunes. Dawson was the town that grew up around the gold hunters and it is still the main town of this region.

Unfortunately, Jack London came back from the Klondike with no gold at all. But it was there that he had an idea for a story called *The Call of the Wild*. It was published in 1903 and became a huge bestseller. *White Fang* was published in 1906 and tells the story of White Fang's attempts to survive as part-dog and part-wolf, in the harsh Northland.

By 1913, Jack London was one of the most highly paid and widely read writers in the world. But sadly he drank too much and wasted his money. In 1916, when he was forty years old, Jack London killed himself.

CHAPTER ONE
The grey cub

It was almost spring in the frozen Northland. Day after day, a she-wolf was searching along the riverbanks — searching for a safe place to give birth to her cubs. She was so heavy that she could not run quickly. And she was so bad-tempered that she snapped at her mate, One Eye, whenever he came close to her.

The she-wolf searched until she found a cave above a small stream. She went through its narrow entrance and crawled along until the walls widened into a little room about six feet across. It was dry and cosy there. The she-wolf circled several times, her nose to the ground. Then, with a tired sigh, she curled her body on the ground.

One Eye laughed at her and wagged his tail. He lay down across the entrance and slept. Soon, the April sunshine began to blaze across the snow. The world was waking up after the long winter. One Eye wanted to go hunting, but when he tried to persuade the she-wolf to go with him, she snarled at him. So he went out alone.

One Eye came back eight hours later. He had caught nothing and was hungrier than when he had set off. He paused at the entrance to the cave and sniffed the air. He could hear strange, faint sounds like muffled sobs. His

mate snarled a warning when he came near. In the morning light, he made out the shape of five cubs. They looked very feeble and helpless.

One cub was different from the others. While his brothers and sisters already showed the reddish tint of their mother, who was part-dog, part-wolf, this cub's hair was grey. He took after his father, One Eye, except that the cub had two eyes!

The grey cub's eyes had not been open for long, but already he could see clearly. His world was only as big as the cave. But he knew that one wall of the cave was different – the mouth of the cave where the light was. He kept crawling towards it, and his mother kept pulling him back.

The grey cub was the fiercest and the strongest of the cubs. By the time he was a month old, he was eating soft meat, half chewed by his mother. Like most creatures of the Wild, the little cub knew hunger. There came a terrible time when there was no more meat and his mother's breasts had no more milk. Then the cubs slept and grew weaker day by day.

One Eye was desperate and searched further and further away from the cave for meat. Even the she-wolf left her cubs and went out to look for food. But when the meat finally came and the grey cub grew strong again, he found that his brothers and sisters were gone.

They had died of hunger. Soon afterwards, there came a time when the cub no longer saw his father going in and out of the cave either. The she-wolf found the remains of his dead body close to a lynx's lair.

The mother lynx was a fierce and bad-tempered creature who was guarding a litter of young kittens. From now on, the she-wolf never went in that direction again. But she knew that the day would come when she would have to face the lynx's anger, for her cub's sake.

By the time his mother was leaving the cave to hunt, the cub had learned an important rule: he must not go near the entrance to the cave. He was afraid to go near it, although he did not know why. But the cub wanted to grow, to experience life, and eventually this instinct swept away his fear and his obedience. One morning, before his mother came back, he moved towards the entrance of his cave.

At first, the bright light outside dazzled him. Then he began to notice the trees, the mountain high above the trees, and the great sky over the mountain. A great fear came upon him as he crouched there, gazing out at the world. His hair stood up on end along his back, and his lips wrinkled weakly as he tried to snarl.

Nothing happened. The cub forgot to be afraid and became curious instead. He stepped outside the cave for the first time.

CHAPTER TWO
Danger outside

The grey cub had lived all his short life on the level floor of a cave. He had never fallen over and been hurt. He did not even know what a fall was. So he stepped outside boldly. Suddenly, he fell forward, and his nose struck the ground. He yelped and rolled down the slope.

The fear came back. At last, the cub stopped rolling. He gave a long, whimpering wail and got up. He was very clumsy! As he walked, he ran into twigs and sticks, and hurt his paws on pebbles and stones. But the longer he walked, the better he walked.

The cub had the luck of a beginner. Born to be a hunter of meat, he came across meat just outside the cave – a nest of chicks. He placed his paw on one. He smelled it. He picked it up in his mouth. It struggled and tickled his tongue. At the same time, the cub felt hunger. His jaws closed together. There was a crunching of bones and warm blood ran in his mouth. The taste was good.

He ate all the chicks. As he crawled away, he met a feathered whirlwind – the mother of the chicks. The beat of her angry wings blinded the cub. He hid his head between his paws and yelped. Then he became angry. He sank his teeth into one of the wings. The need to kill was

upon him. Now he would now destroy a big live thing.

But the mother bird pecked his nose hard until he let go. He turned tail and ran back to the stream. The cub had never seen water before. It was flat, like the floor of the cave, and he stepped on to it. He went under the water, crying with fear, down into the unknown. Then he came to the top and began to swim.

What adventures the grey cub had that day! Not only was his body tired, but his little brain was tired too. How lonely he suddenly felt! He started to look for the cave and his mother.

As the cub moved through the bushes, he saw a flash of yellow. It was a weasel, a small animal that did not frighten him at all. Then he saw a tiny weasel at his feet. He turned it over with his paw. It squeaked. The next moment, the flash of yellow came back. He felt a hard blow on the side of his neck. Then the mother-weasel was at his throat, her teeth buried in his hair and skin.

At first the cub tried to fight; but he was very young, and this was only his first day in the world. He tried to escape. The weasel held on tightly, trying to cut open the vein in his neck so that she could drink his blood.

He thought he was going to die.

The grey cub would have died, but just then his mother came running through the bushes. The weasel let go of the cub and tried to get hold of his mother's throat. But the she-wolf jerked her head and flung the weasel high into the air, then caught it in her teeth. The she-wolf licked her cub's cuts. Then they ate the weasel. And after that, they went back to the cave and slept.

Famine came to the land again. The she-wolf hunted night and day, but caught little. Now the cub did not hunt for play, he hunted to live. He grew wiser and stronger and more confident – and more hungry!

At last, the famine was over for the cub because his mother brought home meat, but a kind of meat he had never tasted before. It was a lynx kitten, partly grown. It was all for him. He did not know how dangerous this was, only that the velvet-furred kitten was meat – and he was happier with every mouthful. Then he slept deeply.

Suddenly, the cub woke up. He had never heard his mother snarl so terribly. Crouching in the mouth of the cave, the cub saw the lynx-mother. The hair rippled up along his back at the sight. He was afraid.

The cub stood by his mother and snarled too. The lynx could not leap into the cave because the entrance was so low; but she crawled in towards them. The cub saw little of the battle between his mother and the lynx. There was a loud snarling and spitting and screeching. Once the cub sprang in and sank his teeth into the hind leg of the lynx. The lynx lashed at him and ripped his shoulder open to the bone.

The fight was long. At last the lynx was dead. But the she-wolf was very weak and sick. For a day and a night, she lay on the ground, hardly breathing. For a week, she never left the cave except for water. She and the cub survived by eating the lynx.

But now the world seemed changed. The cub was more confident. He began to hunt meat with his mother. In this way, he learned the rule of meat. The aim of life was meat. Life lived on life. There were the eaters, and the eaten. The rule of meat was simple: EAT, OR BE EATEN.

CHAPTER THREE

The makers of fire

The cub came across them suddenly – the makers of fire. One morning, heavy with sleep, he ran down to the stream to drink. He knew the trail well. He went that way often and nothing had ever happened to him.

As he was trotting between the trees, he saw and smelt them. Squatting before him were five live things. The cub had never seen such things before. It was his first glimpse of humans. He was puzzled. At the sight of him, the five men did not spring to their feet, nor show their teeth at him, nor snarl. They did not even move, but sat there, silent and frightening.

The cub did not move either. If he had been fully grown, he would have run away. He wanted to run, but a new feeling stopped him. He was overcome by a sense of his weakness and littleness. These live things were powerful, far more powerful than he was.

The cub had never seen a human, but he knew from instinct that Man was the animal that ruled the Wild. Man was the two-legged animal that was master over living things. Fear and respect filled him.

One of the Indians got up and walked over to him. The cub cowered closer to the ground. His hair bristled, his lips stretched back and his little fangs were bared. A hand hesitated above him. Then the man spoke, laughing, "Wabam wabisca ip pit tah." ("Look! The white fangs!").

The other Indians laughed loudly and told the man to pick up the cub. As the hand came closer and closer, a battle raged inside the cub. Should he fight? Or should he give in? He did both! The cub stayed still until the hand almost touched him. Then he fought, his teeth flashing and sinking into the hand. The next moment, a blow on the head knocked him on to his side.

All the fight went out of him.

The cub sat up on his hind legs and wailed. The man was angry and hit the cub again. And he sat up again and wailed more loudly. The Indians laughed and stood in a circle around him. He wailed in terror and hurt. Then he heard a noise. He knew what it was, and he sat silent, waiting for his mother to reach him.

The she-wolf was snarling as she ran towards her cub. The man-animals stood back quickly as she stood over him. She faced the men, with bristling hair, a snarl rumbling deep in her throat.

Suddenly, a cry came from one of the men, Grey Beaver. "Kiche!" he called in surprise. The cub felt his mother soften at the sound. "Kiche!" the man called again sharply.

And then the cub saw his mother, the fearless one, crouch down until her belly touched the ground. She whimpered and wagged her tail, and made signs of peace. The cub could not understand. He was shocked.

"Kiche was my brother's dog," Grey Beaver said. "It is a year since she ran away. Her father was a wolf."

"She must have been living with the wolves," another man said.

"Yes, you can see that the cub's father was also a wolf," Grey Beaver replied, "because his fangs are white. White Fang shall be his name. I have spoken. He is my dog now. For Kiche was my brother's dog, and my brother is dead."

Grey Beaver tied Kiche to a tree. White Fang followed her and lay down beside her. One of the Indians stroked his back and tickled his ears.

Later, White Fang heard strange noises, man-animal noises. The rest of the Indian tribe appeared, about forty of them – and many dogs. All the dogs carried heavy bags on their backs. White Fang had never seen dogs before. When he saw them, he felt that they were his own kind, only somehow different.

When the dogs saw the cub and his mother, they behaved like wolves. They rushed at them wildly. White Fang fell down under them, feeling their sharp teeth on his body. He bit the bellies above him. He could hear the snarl of Kiche as she fought for him. Soon he was on his feet again as the Indians beat the dogs back.

When the Indians moved on, a tiny man-animal took the end of a stick and led Kiche, followed by White Fang. White Fang did not like it. He wanted freedom again.

The Indians put up their tepees by the river. White Fang was afraid of them – they were so tall and they made a loud flapping noise when the wind blew. At last, he dared to go close to one. His nose touched the canvas. He tugged. Nothing happened, so he tugged harder. Nothing happened, except for a scream of a man-animal inside. He was not afraid now.

Later that day, White Fang came across Grey Beaver, squatting on the ground next to a pile of sticks. Suddenly, he saw a strange thing like mist rising from the sticks. Then a live thing appeared, twisting and turning,

the colour of the sun. White Fang crawled towards it. Then his nose touched the flame and his little tongue went out to it. He sat still with terror as the thing held him painfully by the nose.

Grey Beaver laughed loudly until everybody else came and laughed. It was the worst hurt the cub had ever known. He cried and cried, and tried to lick his nose; but his tongue was also burned. He ran to Kiche who was raging at the end of her rope, the only one not laughing at him. He lay next to her, suddenly longing for the quiet of the cave and the stream.

But in the midst of his unhappiness, White Fang knew how powerful the man-animals were. They made life spring from pieces of wood! They were fire-makers!

CHAPTER FOUR
Friendless!

Every day brought new experiences for White Fang. As his mother was tied to her stick for most of the day, he explored the Indian camp alone. The more he came to know the man-animals, the more powerful they seemed. When they walked past, he got out of their way. When they called, he came. When they threatened him, he was afraid. He belonged to them as all the dogs belonged to them.

But this did not happen in a single day. White Fang did not easily give up his memories of the Wild. There were days when he crept to the edge of the forest and stood and listened to something far away calling him. He always went back to the camp unhappy and restless and whimpered at Kiche's side.

The biggest problem in White Fang's life was a dog called Lip-lip. He was larger, older and stronger – and he had chosen White Fang as his victim. Whenever White Fang strayed away from his mother, the bully appeared. If there were no men nearby, he sprang on him to force a fight. And he always won.

This had a bad effect on White Fang. He had to hide his playful, puppyish side all the time, especially when

Lip-lip would not let him play with the other puppies. At feeding time, Lip-lip always made sure that White Fang did not receive enough meat or fish. So the cub learned to become a clever and cunning thief.

The day came at last when Grey Beaver freed Kiche from her rope. White Fang was delighted with his mother's freedom. He went with her everywhere, and, as long as she was there, Lip-lip kept his distance.

One day, White Fang and his mother strayed to the edge of the woods next to the camp. White Fang tried to lead her further on. The quiet woods were calling to him and he wanted her to come with him. He ran on a few steps, stopped and looked back at her. His mother had not moved. He whined, ran back and licked her face, then ran back towards the woods.

Still his mother did not move. She heard a louder call – the call of the fire, the call of Man. Kiche turned and trotted slowly back towards the camp. White Fang sniffed the smell of the pine trees, remembering his old life of freedom. But he was still only a puppy. The call of his mother was stronger than the call of the Wild. And so he got up and trotted after her.

Then came the day when White Fang saw his mother taken aboard a canoe. Grey Beaver had given Kiche to a friend who was making a long journey up the Mackenzie river. When White Fang saw the canoe pull

away with his mother inside, he jumped into the river and swam after it.

Grey Beaver set out in his canoe to fetch White Fang. He reached down into the water and lifted him up by the neck. He held him in the air and beat him. White Fang swung backwards and forwards. He yelped in fear and surprise, then in anger. He snarled, but the blows came faster and heavier.

At last, White Fang stopped struggling and Grey Beaver threw him to the bottom of the canoe. Picking up his paddle, the Indian kicked the cub out of the way. In that moment, White Fang's anger came back. He sank his teeth into the Indian's foot.

Grey Beaver's anger was terrible. Now he used the paddle as well as his hand to beat White Fang. The cub's small body was bruised and sore. That day, he learned a lesson. Whatever happened, he must never bite the man who was lord and master over him.

Lip-lip watched all this from the riverbank. When White Fang was thrown ashore, he ran over and bit him. But Grey Beaver kicked Lip-lip away. That night, White Fang cried for his mother and woke Grey Beaver up. Another beating! He never made such a noise again, except by the edge of the woods. Only the thought of his mother stopped him from running back to the woods. He wanted to be there when she came back to him.

With Kiche gone, Lip-lip made life difficult for White Fang again. The cub found himself friendless in the camp. All the young dogs followed Lip-lip. White Fang was different and they sensed it. They were all afraid of the wild wolf in him. White Fang became a thief, a sneak, a troublemaker, and nobody stopped to wonder why.

The dogs always teased White Fang in a pack. However, he learned two important things by having to fight a pack – how to stay on his feet all the time and how to hurt a dog quickly and by surprise, before all the other dogs ran to help.

White Fang also attacked his enemies if he caught one of them alone. One day, he came across one of the dogs at the edge of the wood. He sprang, bit his throat and killed him. There was a great row in the camp that night, and White Fang would have been put to death if Great Beaver had not saved him.

From that time on, both man and dog hated White Fang. The men cursed and beat him, the dogs snarled at him. White Fang was always nervous and tense, always ready for attack. He knew no love and no kindness. Day by day, he became quicker and more cruel, fiercer and more intelligent. If he had not, he would have died.

And during all this terrible time he waited for his mother to come back.

CHAPTER FIVE
Sledge dog

One cold, autumn day, the Indians started to pack away their summer camp. White Fang watched some of the canoes disappearing down the river. The thought came into his head immediately.

He could be free at last!

Hiding his scent in the stream, White Fang crept into the wood and hid.

"White Fang! White Fang! Come here!" Grey Beaver's voice called angrily.

White Fang trembled, but he did not move. At last, the voices stopped and he crawled out of his hiding place. He played among the trees. How free and alive he felt at last! Then darkness fell. Quite suddenly, he felt lonely. White Fang listened to the silence of the forest and felt danger everywhere. The looming trees and dark shadows terrified him. Then it was cold and he could not snuggle up against a warm tepee. The frost was at his feet and he kept lifting one paw, then the other. White Fang was hungry and he remembered the meat and fish thrown to him by the warm fire.

How soft he had become! He no longer knew how to look after himself in the Wild. The noises of the forest frightened White Fang and he longed for the protection of the Indians. He ran from the forest towards the village.

But he had forgotten. It had gone away.

White Fang came to the place where Grey Beaver's tepee had stood. He sat down and pointed his nose at the moon. His opened his mouth, and in a heart-broken cry, he remembered all his loneliness and fear, his mother, all his past unhappiness. It was the long wolf-howl, the first howl he had ever given.

In the morning, White Fang did not feel so afraid, although he was still lonely. He decided to search for the Indian trail. He followed the riverbank down the stream. All day he ran. He did not rest. He climbed high mountains and sometimes he walked over thin ice.

White Fang ran for thirty hours without stopping. He had not eaten for forty hours and he was weak with hunger. His feet were bruised and bleeding. To make matters worse, snow began to fall, a slippery snow that slowed him down.

Night fell. White Fang, whimpering softly as he limped along, came upon a fresh trail in the snow. Then the camp sounds came to his ears. He saw the blaze of the fire and Grey Beaver crouching over a piece of meat.

White Fang moved slowly towards the firelight. Grey Beaver saw him. White Fang crawled until he lay at his master's feet. Of his own choice he came to sit by man's fire. He trembled and waited for the first blow. It did not fall. Grey Beaver broke the lump of meat in half and gave him a piece. White Fang ate. Then Grey Beaver called for more meat and guarded him from the other dogs as he ate. And White Fang dozed happily by the fire.

Towards the middle of December, when White Fang was eight months old, Grey Beaver went on a journey up the river. He drove one sledge and borrowed a smaller one for his son, Mit-sah, pulled by a team of puppies. White Fang was harnessed to this sledge. There were seven puppies in the team, about nine and ten months old. The puppies were tied with different lengths of rope, so they fanned out from the sledge. In this way, no dog trod in another's footsteps, and no dog could attack the

one in front. If a dog attacked a dog behind him, he would have to turn to face Mit-sah's whip.

Mit-sah had seen Lip-lip's cruelty to White Fang. Now that he was in charge of the puppies, he wanted to teach Lip-lip a lesson. He put him on the longest rope. He also gave Lip-lip extra meat so that the other dogs hated him. As soon as the sled started, the dogs chased him, biting him if ever his long rope went slack. If he turned to face his attackers, Mit-sah whipped him.

White Fang was happy in his new work although he never did learn to play with the rest of the pack. He only knew how to fight. He was master of them, and they knew it. He would eat his meat quickly, then snatch the meat from the other dogs. White Fang became stronger on that long journey. He saw the world as fierce and brutal, a world without warmth.

White Fang never grew to like the hands of the man-animals. They gave meat, but more often they gave hurt. He felt no love for Grey Beaver, although he respected him. To have a master, he had to serve that master by protecting him and his possessions. White Fang acted out of duty, not out of love.

And he knew that if ever he met his mother again, he would not desert his master to go with her.

CHAPTER SIX

Older and wiser

It was April when Grey Beaver finished his long journey. White Fang was one year old when he pulled the sledge back into the home village. He no longer feared the dogs who had teased him the year before.

One of these dogs was called Baseek. When White Fang was eating a large piece of meat, Baseek rushed at him. White Fang slashed Baseek twice, dropping the meat on the ground. As the other dog bent his head to smell it, White Fang struck him again. With the first slash, he ripped Baseek's ear to ribbons. Then he knocked Baseek off his feet, biting his throat and shoulder. The old dog turned his back on the meat and walked away.

White Fang was very proud of himself. He did not look for trouble, but now he had the right to walk about without being attacked. The older dogs accepted him as an equal. They left him alone.

In midsummer, White Fang met his mother again.

He remembered her. But Kiche did not remember him. When White Fang ran over to her, she snarled and cut his cheek with her teeth. It was not Kiche's fault. A wolf-mother is made to forget her older cubs so that she can give all her attention to her new cubs.

One of these puppies now came up to White Fang. He sniffed the little animal. Kiche ran up to him and ripped his face for the second time. White Fang went away. The old memories died down again. His mother was not important in his life, and he was not important in hers. He allowed Kiche to drive him away.

In the third year of White Fang's life, a great famine came to the Indians. There had been few fish in the summer. In the winter, the deer did not come to their usual place. Only the strong survived. The Indians chewed their leather moccasins and mittens, and even ate some of their dogs. The dogs began to eat one another.

In this terrible time, White Fang went into the woods. He had a better chance of survival there than the dogs in the camp. He was very good at catching small animals, as he had learned when he was a cub. Sometimes, he robbed the animal traps the Indians had put down. He even took a rabbit from Grey Beaver's trap.

Soon he left that part of the country to search for food and travelled to the valley where he was born. Here, in the cave, he came across Kiche once again. It was at this time that he saw Lip-lip who had also taken to the woods in his search for food. White Fang bristled and snarled. He did not waste any time. White Fang struck his old enemy and rolled him on his back. Then he sank his teeth into Lip-lip's thin throat and killed him.

One day, not long after, he came to the edge of the forest where the ground sloped down to the Mackenzie river. He heard the sounds of voices. Still hidden in the trees, White Fang stopped to look. He knew those sounds. It was his old village in a new place. He sniffed the air – fish! There was food again!

White Fang came out boldly from the forest and trotted into the camp straight to Grey Beaver's tepee.

"White Fang!" Grey Beaver's wife called, "you've come back. Here's some fish for you!" She threw him a whole, fresh fish. White Fang ate it all. Then he lay down to wait for his master.

During the spring of 1898, when White Fang was almost five years old, Grey Beaver decided to make another long journey. "There are thousands of gold-hunters using the Yukon river," he told the others. "I shall go to Fort Yukon and sell furs and mittens and moccasins. These men from the south never bring enough warm clothes with them."

Grey Beaver made more money than he had ever dreamed about. And like a true Indian, he settled down to trade carefully and slowly.

"I do not mind if it takes the rest of the summer and the winter to sell all my goods," he told himself happily.

It was at Fort Yukon that White Fang saw his first white man. Just as the Indian tepees had seemed powerful to him, so did the houses and the huge fort of the white man. Here was power. These white masters were strong, and Grey Beaver was like a child among them.

And it was a white man who brought misery to White Fang.

CHAPTER SEVEN

Beauty Smith

White Fang slunk around the white men and saw that they did not harm their dogs. And they were curious about him. His wolfish appearance caught their eye. White Fang watched and learned. Very few white men lived in this place all the time, but every two or three days, a large steamer stopped at the fort. White men got off. Then, a few hours later, they went away on it again.

Some of the men brought their dogs ashore. The white men's dogs did not seem to be very powerful. They were all shapes and sizes. And none of them knew how to fight.

White Fang fought with them – he knew no better. They were soft and helpless, and they made too much noise. Killing them became his work. He hung around, waiting for the steamer to come in. He had learned long ago that the Indians were angry when their dogs were killed. The white men on the steamer were no different. When White Fang slashed the dogs' throats and left them for the Indian dogs to tear to pieces, the men rushed in with their guns.

The white men who lived in Fort Yukon did not like the strangers who came on the steamer. So they enjoyed the trouble that White Fang caused the new arrivals. They always came down to the river to watch the fun.

One man was always the first there when the steamer arrived. The other men called him 'Beauty'. Why? Because he was not beautiful, of course! Beauty Smith was a small man with a small, pointed head. His jaw was so enormous that it seemed to rest on his chest. His thin neck could hardly hold up such a heavy load. His teeth were large and yellow. His hair was thin and yellow. Yellow also described the man – he was a coward.

This was the man who wanted to own White Fang. But White Fang always bared his teeth at him and backed away. He did not like the man. The feel of him was bad. White Fang sensed the evil in him.

One day, Beauty Smith came to Grey Beaver's camp. White Fang slid away to the edge of the camp. He could see the man and Grey Beaver talking together.

"No!" Grey Beaver said. "I cannot sell my dog. There is no dog like him on the Yukon. He fights. He is the strongest sledge dog I have. No, I cannot sell him."

But Beauty Smith was cunning. He brought whisky for Grey Beaver day after day. "I'll give you whisky in return for White Fang," Beauty Smith said.

"You catch 'im, you take 'im," Grey Beaver muttered at last.

"You catch him," Beauty Smith replied.

White Fang came back into the camp as soon as Beauty Smith left. Grey Beaver staggered over to him and tied a piece of leather around his neck. When Beauty Smith came back later, he put out his hand to stroke him. White Fang struck with his fangs. Beauty pulled away his hand, just in time, frightened and angry.

Beauty Smith took the end of the leather and walked away. White Fang did not get up, even when the leather was tight. Grey Beaver hit him hard. White Fang obeyed, hurling himself upon the stranger. But his new master was ready. He swung his stick and smashed White Fang on to the ground. Grey Beaver laughed and nodded.

White Fang knew that the white man was more powerful than him. He did not fight. He followed Beauty Smith to the fort, his tail between his legs, snarling softly. White Fang was tied to a bed. Within an hour, he chewed through the leather and went back to Grey Beaver. Beauty Smith fetched him back. But this time, his new owner beat him with a club and a whip. It was the worst beating White Fang had ever had.

Beauty Smith tied White Fang to a stick. All night long, White Fang chewed through the stick, until he trotted back in the early morning to Grey Beaver. Beauty Smith came to fetch him again! This time, Grey Beaver watched while the white man raised his whip to White Fang.

"I cannot protect you, White Fang," he muttered sadly, "because you no longer belong to me."

When the beating was over, Beauty Smith dragged White Fang back to the fort and chained him up. And while he was there, Grey Beaver left the Yukon.

White Fang remained at Fort Yukon. His new owner was half mad. But what did a dog know about such things? White Fang knew only that Beauty Smith was a powerful man, and that he would have to obey him.

CHAPTER EIGHT
The fighter

Thanks to Beauty Smith, White Fang became the enemy of everyone, and a much fiercer enemy than he had ever been. He was chained inside a wooden cage at the back of the fort. Here men came to tease him and laugh at him, knowing that he hated to be laughed at. White Fang hated everything, but most of all, he hated Beauty Smith.

By this time, White Fang was terrifying. Five feet in length and two and a half feet high, he weighed over ninety pounds. One day, Beauty Smith took the chain from White Fang's neck. White Fang ran around his cage, trying to get out. Suddenly, the door of the cage opened. Something unusual was happening. The door opened wider. Then a huge dog was pushed inside and the door was slammed shut.

White Fang had never seen such a dog before, but he was not afraid. He sprang forward, ripping open the dog's neck. The men outside the cage shouted and clapped. There was no hope for the other dog, and finally its owner dragged its body outside. Beauty Smith made plenty of money on bets that day.

White Fang had to fight every day after that, and sometimes as much as three times a day. He became known as the 'Fighting Wolf'. In the autumn, when the first snows were falling, Beauty Smith decided to go to the town of Dawson, where gold-hunters worked. The men paid in gold dust to see White Fang fight. He was given no rest. He was kept angry most of the time. His early training, when he fought with Lip-lip and the other puppies, now paid off. No dog could make White Fang fall to the ground. He knew more about fighting than any of the dogs that came to fight him.

As time went by, there were fewer and fewer fights. The men were tired of seeing their dogs killed. What did Beauty Smith do? He brought wolves, trapped in the forest by Indians, to fight White Fang.

One day, a fully-grown lynx was brought to fight him. Then White Fang fought for his life. The lynx was as fast and as strong as him. White Fang won but that was the end of the fighting because there were no more animals to bring – until a man called Tim Keenan arrived with the first bulldog ever seen in that part of the country.

For a week, there was talk of nothing else except the fight that would take place between White Fang and Cherokee. But when Beauty Smith slipped the chain from White Fang's neck, White Fang did not attack straight away. He had never seen such a strange dog before. Cherokee waddled forward and blinked at White Fang.

"Go to him, Cherokee! Eat 'im up, Cherokee!" the crowd shouted. But Cherokee was lazy. And he was not used to fighting. Tim Keenan pushed his dog forward. Cherokee began to growl, which made the hair rise on White Fang's neck and shoulders. At last, Cherokee began to run towards his enemy.

Then White Fang struck. He slashed with his fangs and jumped clear. The bulldog was bleeding from a rip in his thick neck, but he turned and followed White Fang. Again and again, White Fang sprang in, slashed the bulldog and got away safely.

The crowd became excited and began to place larger bets. But White Fang had a problem. He could not get to the soft underside of the bulldog's throat. The dog was

too short and its huge jaw protected it. White Fang darted in and out, unharmed, always hurting the other. The time went by. White Fang still danced on, leaping in and out, while the bulldog followed him. Time and time again, White Fang tried to knock the dog off his feet, but he was already too close to the ground to make any difference. Suddenly, he saw the chance to strike at Cherokee's shoulder. But as he did so, his own shoulder was too high above the bulldog's short body.

For the first time in his fighting history, men saw White Fang fall over.

In that moment, as White Fang turned a half-somersault in the air, Cherokee's teeth closed around his throat. White Fang sprang to his feet and tried to shake off the bulldog. Round and round he went, whirling and turning, hating the fifty pound weight dragging at his throat. White Fang was tired. He could do nothing, and he could not understand it. Never, in all his fighting, had such a thing happened. All that saved White Fang from death was the loose skin of his neck and the thick fur that covered it.

Beauty Smith took a step towards White Fang and began to laugh. White Fang went wild with anger. But the harder he tried to shake off Cherokee, the tighter Cherokee's grip became.

Cherokee was slowly strangling White Fang.

CHAPTER NINE

A new friend

"Cherokee! Cherokee! Cherokee!" the crowd called.

Beauty Smith sprang upon White Fang and began to kick him. Suddenly, there were noises from the crowd. A tall, young man was pushing his way through. He walked right up to Beauty Smith and hit him in the face with his fist. "You cowards!" he shouted at the crowd. "You animals!"

The man hit Beauty Smith once more. "You animal!" he said again. "Come on, Matt, lend a hand," he called to his friend. Both men bent over the dogs and tried to pull them apart.

"It's no use, Mr Scott; you can't break 'em apart that way. He ain't bleeding much. Ain't got all the way in yet," Matt said.

Scott turned to the crowd. "Won't some of you help?" he cried.

But no help was offered. Tim Keenan tapped Mr Scott on the shoulder. "Don't break my dog's teeth, stranger," he said angrily.

"Then I'll break his neck," Scott answered.

He looked at Tim Keenan coldly. "Your dog?" he asked.

The owner grunted.

"Then get in here and break this grip," Scott said.

"Well, I don't know how, stranger," Tim Keenan said slowly.

"Then get out of my way," Scott replied, "and don't bother me. I'm busy."

At last, he managed to loosen the jaws a bit at a time with the muzzle of his gun. "Get ready to receive your dog!" he called to Cherokee's owner. "Now!"

Tim Keenan dragged Cherokee back into the crowd. Weedon Scott looked down at White Fang. "Matt, how much is a good sledge-dog worth?" he asked.

"Three hundred dollars," his friend told him.

"And for a dog that's mangled up like this one?" he asked.

"Half of that," Matt said.

Scott turned to Beauty Smith. "Did you hear, Mr Beast? I'm going to take your dog from you, and I'm going to give you a hundred and fifty dollars for him."

He handed over the money. Beauty Smith refused to take it. "I ain't selling," he said.

"Oh yes, you are," Scott said, "because I'm buying. Here's your money. The dog's mine. Or do I have to hit you again?"

"All right," Beauty Smith said, trembling with fear, "but a man's got his rights."

"That's true," Scott said, handing over the money again. "A man's got his rights. But you're not a man. You're a beast."

The crowd began to leave.

"Who is that man?" Tim Keenan asked.

"Weedon Scott," someone answered.

"And who in hell is Weedon Scott?" Tim Keenan asked angrily.

"A gold mining expert," the man answered. "If you want to keep out of trouble, you'll steer clear of him."

White Fang tried to get up, but his legs were too weak to hold him. He sank back into the snow, his eyes half-closed and his tongue hanging limp. He looked like a dog that had been strangled.

"It's hopeless," Weedon Scott sighed a few days later as he sat on the step of his log cabin watching White Fang. "He's even wilder than when we rescued him. He's a wolf and there's no taming him."

"I wouldn't say that," Matt said. "Wolf or dog, it's all the same. He's been tamed already. You can see the marks of sledge ropes across his chest. Take my advice and turn him loose for a while."

Weedon Scott took off White Fang's chain. "Poor devil," Scott said, "he doesn't know what to do now he's free. He needs some human kindness."

He went into his cabin and came out with a piece of

meat. He threw it to White Fang who just looked at it suspiciously. Another dog rushed to get it. White Fang killed him in a flash.

"Perhaps it would be kinder to kill him," Scott said, "since we can't tame him."

"Give 'im a fair chance, Mr Weedon," Matt said. "This is the first time he's been let loose."

Weedon Scott began to talk to White Fang, softly and gently. Then he held out a piece of meat. White Fang refused to touch it. There was danger lurking behind that piece of meat. In the end, the man tossed the meat on the snow at White Fang's feet. White Fang smelled it, keeping his eyes on the man. Nothing happened. He took the meat into his mouth and swallowed it. Nothing happened. The man threw him another piece of meat!

The next time, the man held out the meat in his hand. White Fang growled, then ate the meat slowly. Nothing happened. Still he waited for the punishment, but the man went on talking softly. White Fang was torn by different feelings. He felt the kindness but he dreaded the punishment. He snarled, but he did not snap with his teeth. The hand came down towards him. It touched the ends of his hair. It stroked him. White Fang growled and growled and waited for the soft voice to become shrill and angry.

"Well, I'll be gosh-swoggled!" Matt said in surprise.

It was the beginning of the end for White Fang – the ending of the old life, the ending of hate. A new and fairer life had begun. Weedon Scott had touched the other side of White Fang's nature, the kind side. White Fang did not run away because he liked this new master. This one was the best yet.

CHAPTER TEN
A home at last

White Fang began to do his duty to his new master. He looked after his log cabin. He learned the difference between good and bad men. Weedon Scott took his job seriously, the job of making up for the harm that men had done to White Fang. He went out of his way to be kind to White Fang. He stroked him every day, and White Fang grew to like this petting. But he never gave up growling.

As the weeks went by, White Fan's liking for his master slowly changed to love. He did not really know what love was, only that he was lonely and unhappy whenever his master was not there.

In the late spring, a great sadness came to White Fang. Without warning, his master went away. A few days later, Matt wrote to Weedon Scott:

'That wolf of yours won't work. Won't eat. Ain't got no life in him. Wants to know what has become of you, and I don't know how to tell him. I think he's gonna die.'

One night, White Fang heard footsteps outside the cabin. The door opened and Weedon Scott came in.

"Where's the wolf?" he asked.

White Fang stood by the stove, watching and waiting. He did not rush forward like other dogs. But he looked at his master with eyes shining with love. And as Weedon Scott stroked him, White Fang snuggled against his master's body.

"Gosh, look at him!" Matt said.

Life flowed through White Fang again. Having learned to snuggle, he could not stop. He had always liked his head to be free – that was the wild animal in him. Now he let himself be helpless in his master's hands.

But White Fang's happiness did not last. He could feel a change in the air – he did not know what it was, only that he did not like it.

"Listen to that!" Matt said one evening. "I do believe that wolf knows that you're going back home!" White Fang was outside the door, whining with anxiety.

"What can I do with a wolf in California?" Weedon Scott said desperately. "He would kill every dog on sight and he'd be taken away from me and shot."

"But how on earth does he know you're going?" Matt asked in amazement.

"It's beyond me," Scott answered, shaking his head.

The terrible day came at last when White Fang saw his master packing his clothes into a bag. White Fang knew what this meant. That night, he pointed his nose to the cold stars and gave the long wolf-howl.

"From the way he was when you went away last time, I think he'll die," Matt remarked.

In the morning, Weedon Scott came to the door and called White Fang. "You poor devil," he whispered, rubbing White Fang's ears. "Now give me a growl – the last goodbye growl." But White Fang refused. Instead, he snuggled up to his master.

Down on the Yukon river came the whistle of the steamer.

"You'd better hurry!" Matt shouted.

Weedon Scott shut the cabin door. From inside came a low whining and sobbing.

"Take good care of him, Matt," Scott said. "Write and let me know how he gets on."

"Listen to that!" Matt cried. White Fang was howling as dogs howl when their masters are dead.

At the gangplank to the steamer, Matt shook hands with his friend. But his hand went limp as his gaze fixed on something in the distance. Scott turned to look. Sitting on the deck of the steamer, several feet away and watching them, was White Fang. He had jumped straight through the window of the cabin and was covered in cuts.

"I'll write to you about him!" Weedon Scott laughed. And he did.

Sierra Vista, California

Dear Matt

White Fang has settled down well. He keeps himself to himself and does not play or fight with the other dogs. He does not really like my children, but he puts up with them for my sake.

But now for my big news! White Fang is famous! A prisoner escaped from jail recently – my father was the judge who sent him there for fifty years. Well, the escaped prisoner broke into our house. He wanted revenge. White Fang killed him, saving my father's life. My wife has named him the Blessed Wolf, and we all call him that now.

Yours, Weedon Scott

At last, White Fang had found a real home.